1

The slow evolution of Dove Night is a compliation or EP of songs written by

Dove Night and David Waterbury. Here is the first song on the track, That is

why I fell in love with you

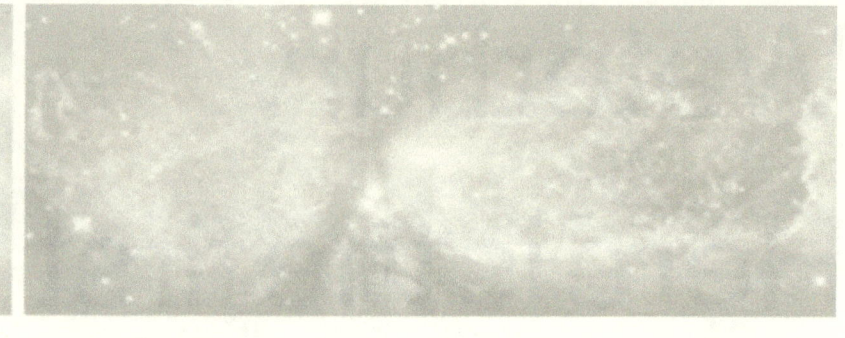

it is why i fell in love w
dove night

That is why I fell in love with you is a song about falling in

love with the right person.

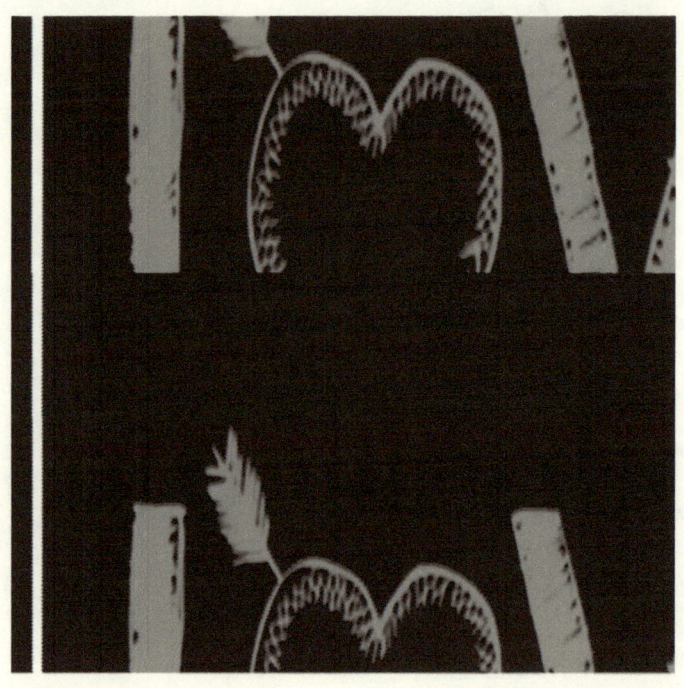

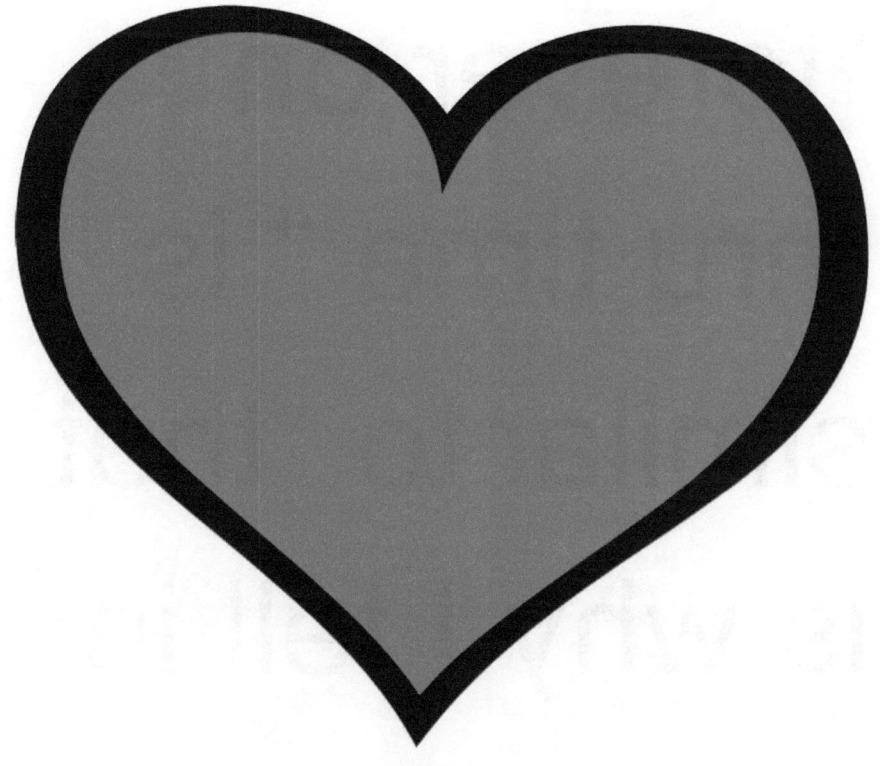

The song "forever on thru time " is similar to "that is why I fell in love with you"in that the person singing has been alone for a while and finally fall in

love with the right person

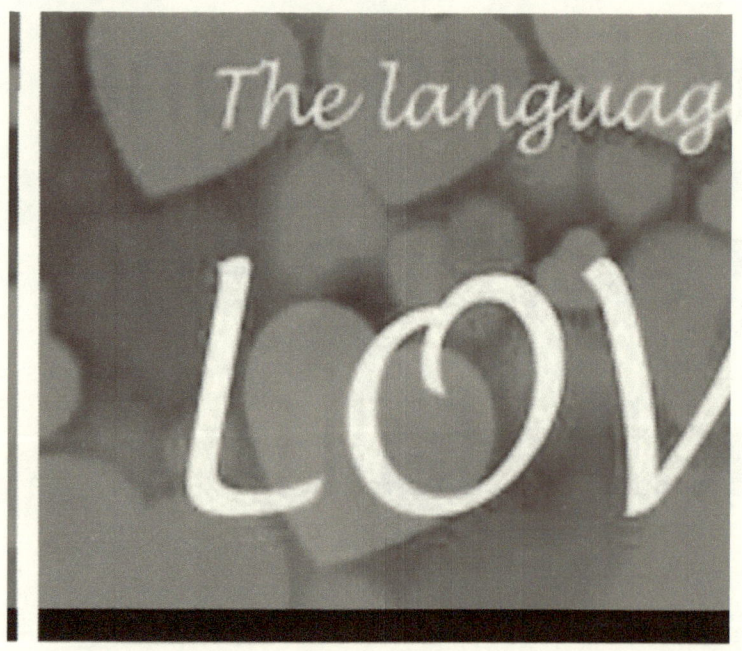

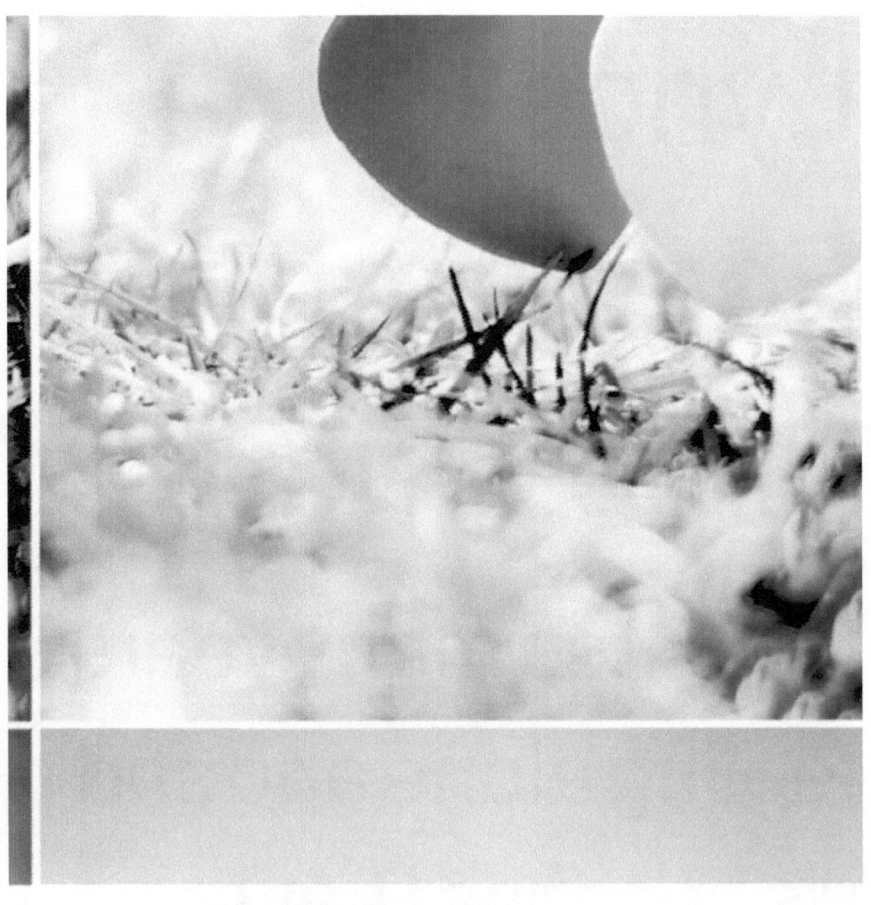

Lyrics to Forever on thru Time-lyrics

I spent so many years feeling alone and sad it's because I never had been loved because I thought I was bad pre

chorus- but then you came into my life and I was am so amazed because you 're all mine forever on thru time

chorus-so I'm happy to be ,by your side because we 'll stay

together forever on
thru time

and when you're not
around , I still feel loved
cause at the end of
the day, you 're always
at home instrumental
intro And There was
a time

when I felt I was dying
In the past, all through
my life ,there was no
one besides me pre
chorus

chorus guitar solo /
instrumental solo
prechorus \\ chorus

instrumental interlude - forever!!!!!!!!!!!!!!

Forever on thru time is a song about finding true love after many years of not finding the right person or being alone. I am one person who spent many years

being alone so the song
is definitely
biographical but many

people can relate to
being alone or
spending many years
with the wrong person.
Sometimes love takes

time and sometimes it
can take years.

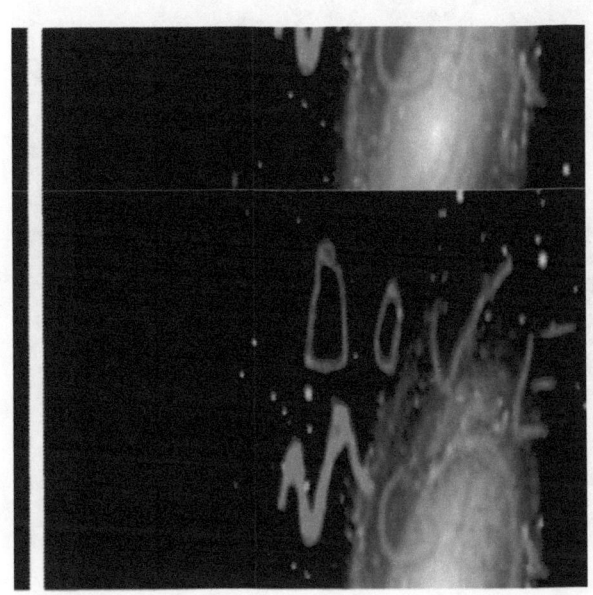

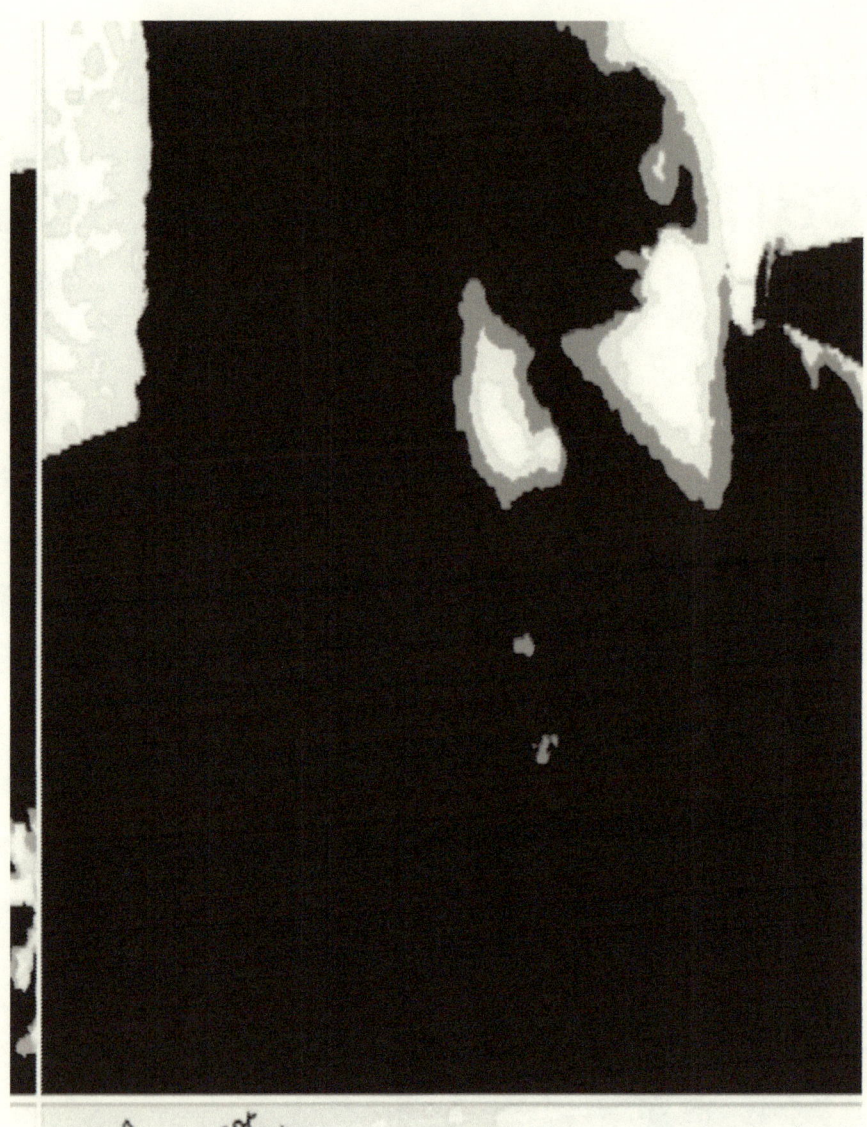

I really want to be with you is a song about telling someone we found love , the song was great to make and it was a joy to sing in the studio and will be a joy to sing it to people in public

Lyrics to I really want
to be with you

I was feeling!
Alone and blue til I met
you
Now I know you feel it
too. No more feeling
blue !!!

We had found love
(2,3,4)

Chorus;

I really want to be with
you because we know
our love is true

I really wanna be with
you

Alright!! – dove vocal
/ break

Now it's getting easy to
see , that you and me
Will be together
forever , for eternity
We had found love
Chorus

Keyboard solo

 Chorus

The end

Song is written by dove
night and dave
Waterbury (BMI inc)

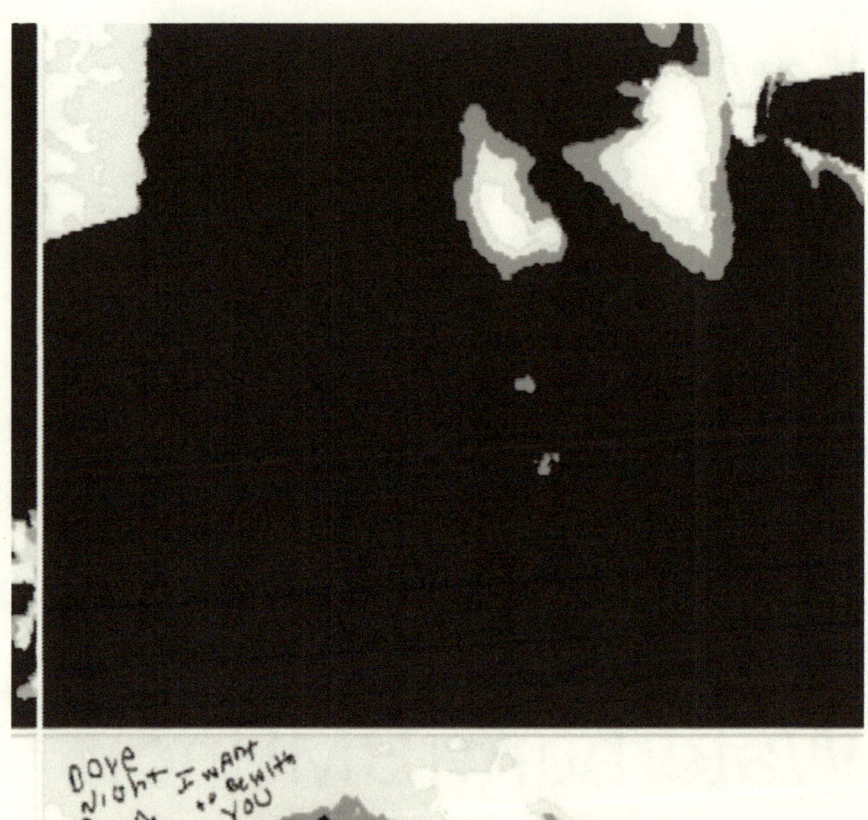

Outcast is about feeling real blue and down. I written after some horrific events I experienced after coming out to LA and living here for almost a year ,homeliness , robbery and the day of

the recording ,
someone died in the
house I was had just
moved into. The man
died of an overdose
and to see that and go
into a recording booth
effected my mood, the
song and the lyrics to

outcast.

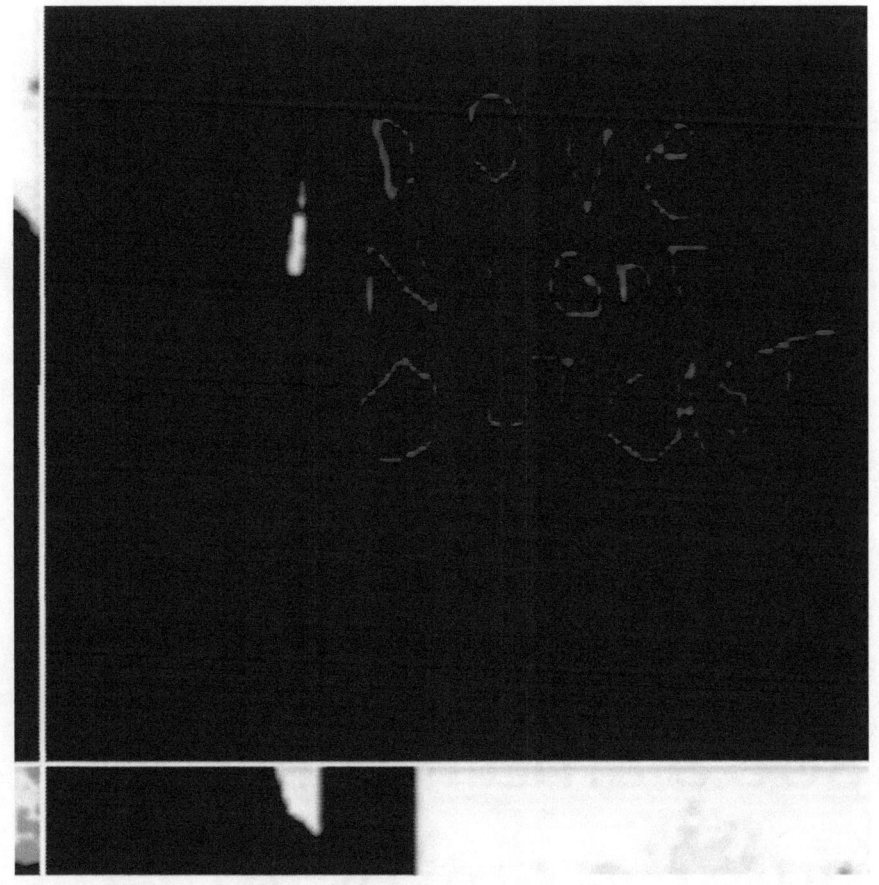

Outcast song

Lyrics

I look around

I look around at my peers

I get stoned, I get put
down in jeers

But I look , I look and
see a small light that
puts me out ,puts me
out of human sight

The sight of being ,the sight of being myself and I cry

Chorus; people don't know what they're going to do . putting someone out because he's fit to chose ,a choser of lies and punches in the face ,the guy aint seen nowhere in the human race. He thinks his life is gone and not meant to last , the guy is just another , another outcast

Break

I remember ,back when
I was fifteen , I was
rejected, I was
considered unclean
when I look , look and
see a small tree, it said
,I 'm no gooder than he
and I'm dead

Chorus

Instrumental solo

I look out,
I look out the window ,I
see nothing of a good
symbol , and I
wonder,and I wonder
where I am , I always
suffered ,always

suffered and ran and I

weak

Chorus

Instrumental solo

/chorus the end

Tragedy is not what I

am is about

redemption and

overcome obstacles
and it is a song that is
positive ,aboutfeeling
sabatoged because of
bad experiences and
then realizing that a
person is no tragedy
and that they have

enough to overcome
any obstacle,

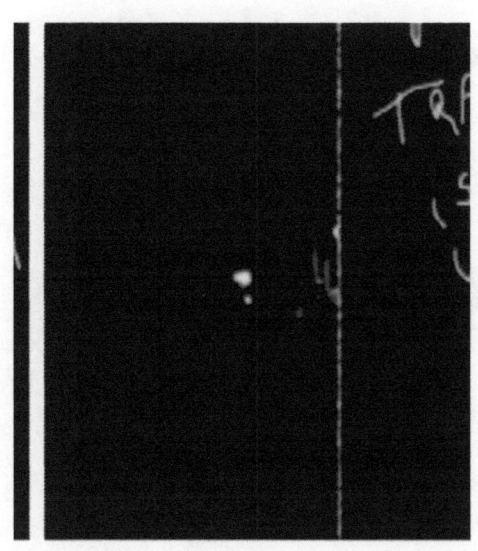

Tragedy is not what I am is a song about not wanting to not be a victim, it is about being a winner, and overcoming obstacles,

AND LAST ONE!
UNIQUE
!!!!!!!!!!!!!!!!!!!!!!!!!

Unique is a song about
my struggles in trying
to make my dreams

come true in the entertainment industry in Hollywood however it is about my struggles and the hope that Hollywood, which is a great town ,will focused entirely on

someone's talent and
not the superficial.

Lyrics to Unique
I had a hard time trying
to make it ,in
Hollywood because of
my image

Record companies,
they had rejected me
but I know ,someone
will sign me

Small instrumental
break

Chorus" I had a hard
life but I overcame it

I am not destined to have my heart broken (2x)

Break

 I had been told by some people that I had to have an afro and be an anorexic

But you see ,It is not meant for me ,because I chose to live in my true reality

chorus I'm unique , I'm unique

I had a hard life but overcame it etc…….(2x)

Take it to bridge- vocal
!

Solo

Chorus :I'm unique, I'm unique - I had a hard life – 4x

 I'm unique , I 'm unique

Dove Night is a singer, songwriter, artist ,musician and intellectual who loves to create, more info,contact Dove at doveneedslove22@yah

[oo.com](oo.com) and @doveneedslove22